Open Skies

Open Skies

Sushma Sagar

PARTRIDGE
A Penguin Random House Company

To order additional copies of this book, contact
Partridge India
000 800 10062 62
www.partridgepublishing.com/india
orders.india@partridgepublishing.com

In memory of my parents Sohanlal and Leela, who had dreams for me and whose belief in me nurtured my sensibilities.

Acknowledgements

I would like to express my gratitude to everyone who encouraged me to continue writing, specially to my two foster children, Gautam and Ritu, who have supported me through thick and thin.

To my friend and confidante Brijinder who is always there whenever I need her.

To my one and only sister Prem for the love she pours upon me, as well as to the rest of the family.

To Bhawna Puri, who encouraged me to publish my work even if it meant having to sell my house!

To Ravneet who prompted me to send one poem to Sensei Ikeda, which led to my receiving a direct word of encouragement from him.

And to several others including Sujata who read my poems appreciatively.

Contents

Index of first lines

Index of first lines

One

A language exists
Ancient as the icy caverns
In Antarctica, not deciphered
By human beings

The trees have always whispered
In it to each other
A simple truth:
That there is joy for the asking,
Abundant as is a rich granary.

Each leaf that flutters in
The daylight breeze glows
With this knowledge
Every hopper and each of the bees
Hovering above the babbling
Stream that flows
Like life itself—each knows.

continued . . .

While Man, Cassandra like, doubts
He lives out his clinquant bouts
Of merriment, to mask
His despondency

If he would listen he would hear
A message, bliss imbued
From the world visible
And would soak in the sunlight
Like some plant, emerald hued
Be nourished as the vital sap gushes
From within the depths
More ancient than
The caverns in Antarctica-
That there is joy for the asking
Abundant as is a rich granary.

Two

The Universe is
Our receptacle divine
Our cosmic urn!
We are the spark
Of consciousness,
In its dark
We could move our life
In a single moment
Towards bliss,
And much we could learn
Of all there is to know

The four winds
As always, blow
Any of the wind-wards
We could turn
Have invisible armies
March along!

To our right
The heavenly lords
To our left, in royal state
Legions of gods
Like warriors
Around a potentate

continued . . .

Would we but heed
Our inner voice
And towards
Self actualization
Proceed!!

A resolve that's strong
A will of steel
Is what we need
To right what's wrong.

No bloodshed! But to bleed
Out all remnants of Hate
Of selfish greed
Of callous unconcern
Of pitiable jealousy
With which
Each one of us can burn
Oh folly!

All these and more
Of things plaguing us
Like some pesky mole!
Could we but
Cleanse them out
Of our human soul

Three

And why should a son be silent?
Silence can seep into the day
One following another, until
A lifetime has vanished away.

And should a son not reply
Nor not declare he is happy!
So much to rejoice about
So much that is good and meant
To bring a sparkle to a mother's eye!

All our miseries may lie hidden
In our ancient or recent memories

So are the beauteous moments.
Surely we each encountered
The pure, the glorious
In our journeys!
The riotous palette
Of seasons gliding by
These choose, and bring to mind

Do you not hear
The tinkling laughter
Of Sarah? . . . And
In your heart a blossom find?

Four

As petals from their blossoms
Withering part
And fall in silence
Upon the earth below
Countless moments of life
Into the air I did throw
Until the Buddha's words
I read with my heart
All is illusion, all is fleeting
Only the One Truth remains
Unchanging everlasting:
The Eternal Law!
I strive now, to break the chains
Of my evil karma
And its negative power
And am emerging from the mire
Like the lotus flower.

Five

Still your self my turbulent mind
And seek the powers that satisfy
The light of the sun sparkles!
It silvers the dome of the sky
It burns to brighten the worlds
As far as visible to the human eye

The gloom's within some deeply dark
Recesses of our selves
Where our past is lodged
Like a foul spirit.
Awaiting a cleansing
Awaiting absolution

A carpenter knocks and chisels
The wooden piece
He is working upon
In order to create utility
And vendors ply.

This racket and din
Is life indeed
It's here that
Joys and sorrows vie
For supremacy in the lives
Of those who exist
In simplicity

Six

There was a clap of thunder
Though not a wispy cloud in sight
The sky suffused a cinnabar red.
I swear I heard a tinkling
As if a cosmic set
Of copper, cattle-bells was shaken
By an invisible, giant hand

A veil was torn asunder!
A robin's sarabande in flight
A pansy's dimpling in its bed
I noticed—My spirit un-crinkling
As if no longer with ennui beset
But had stirred its self to awaken
. . . . and expand

Seven

It is not possible for me to soar like an eagle
What is possible is for me is to love the Earth
Upon which I walk and to give it back
All that it gives me and a little more,
Within my capacity

I cannot help it if I am not brilliantly cerebral
But I can help to be the best
At what I have chosen to do
With my time on earth

I cannot help it if people betray me.
Mock me, deride me or ignore my existence
What I can help is to seek the grace to forbear
And each day scatter into the air
The ashes of my afflictions
And thereby let go of them.

I cannot help the way I look, but I can help rejoice.
In being what I am, reflecting in myself
The silent dignity of the cosmos,
Firm in the belief
That the indestructible Eternal Spirit
Is within me, as it is in all else.

continued . . .

I cannot help it if I am black,
Brown, yellow or white
What I can be is to absorb
In myself the color of Truth
And live in its rainbow hues.

I cannot help it if I am not tall and shapely
What I can help is to see beauty within my core;
To savor the glory of everything in creation
And revel in it all.

I cannot help it if I am not everlasting
What I can help is to accept my transience;
To look at Death, as my repose,
And as my rejuvenator

I cannot help it if the rungs of the ladder
I am climbing, are too many
But I can prevent myself looking down
At the people that are following in my wake
And assess my worth as great;
Or to look up
And be dismayed how many are above me.

continued . . .

I can erase envy from my thoughts and spit out
The bitter taste of being pushed to the periphery
I can be content instead to stand upon the riverbank,
In unity with all that lives alongside me,
In quietude and cheer

I cannot help growing old, but I can help
To garner wisdom as I move along the road of life
And to continue to play my role in making this world
A better place, as a result of my sojourn here

Eight

A rill frolics down
Through crevice,
Over boulders creaming
It plops, it ripples,
It drips down leaf-nipples

The flow of life within my skin,
Countless beings
In awesome unity streaming!

Hammock wrapped, and dreaming
My tiny human form swings
Awaiting Job like for the
Stream to sing me a song
I could borrow, make it my own

And Creation draws near
Aware, awake, a-beaming

Nine

The words that leave my mouth
For others to hear
Are mere sounds
Unless my own heart is listening
The sanctum of my mind too is listening

We seek meaning at all times
In the lexicon of existence
Huge words: Truth, Eternity
Life, Death!
And how casually we use them!

As if they are simple and straight
As a syzygy

As if each of these elusive realities
Can be grasped
And then cast away at will.

While even the creature that
Walks about inside
My skin is a mystery to me

Ten

At last, I found it!
The gem in my robe-hem
Not a myth, not a fable, I learn
It's a fabulous diadem!
My human Entity
Bedizened by the mystic
Power eterne

The Self that is my essence
Is a wondrous being
With joy in her heart
A dance in her toes
A song on her tongue

The strength to believe
I will, and therefore I can
I am of the ocean a
Priceless drop
Carrying the ocean within me

continued . . .

I breathe happiness
I speak courage
I carry no useless
Burdens of sorrow or regret

Have boarded the ship
The Great Seer built
For all who dwell on this earth
I am on the way
Unfolding my destiny
Born to create beauty
And . . . . worth.

Eleven

Does an elixir
A magic wheel,
Or Solomon's seal
Exist,
With which to crystallize
The dreams we dream?

This world is our own creation
I weep over its state
How powerless I feel
Flung about by what I believe is fate
In truth, by my own passions innate
And how easily I succumb
To avarice or hate
Creating my travails

Whatever be my faith
Whether in cycles of
Birth and death
Or in any theism great
I am still the one who creates
My self and this world
In which I have taken breath.

Twelve

Did I not get you right beloved Life?
I read you Darkness

My deluded mind pronounced you indifferent

But you are thoroughly involved with me
Primed you are to fulfill
My every creative need
You respond !

Yes, you respond to this thinking reed

Thirteen

Let the storm blow so hard
The treetops humbled, bow
Let the elements come to grips
Setting the skies aquiver
Let raindrops fall like arrowheads
Upon the face of the river

The one who stands strong as a rock
That lights the way for sailing ships
Will neither bend nor shiver!

His gaze is steady upon the waves
Inundating the weary
Each tiny vessel he treats
With care, calmly guiding all
He wavers not, the blasts he braves
He knows he must deliver

Fourteen

Abruptly the light receded
The stars gathered up their sparks
And vanished
And the Universe that had been
Whispering courage in my ear
Stepped back to view me
From its distant Infinity
The birdcalls were silenced
The landscape darkened and stilled
And Hope that had taken infant steps
Into my heart, froze midway . . . . .
It retracted

I was left to watch the slow unveiling
Of my existence, in all my trivial
Fears and anxieties

Fifteen

Strive for victory.
Never give up
Face life sanguinely.
Respect your self and others
Believe in your ability to change for the better,
Illimitably
Trust in the goodness of humanity.
Be sincere about your beliefs
And in your words

Actively seek to become wiser
Live each day as if it were your last
Create value ceaselessly
Look for that which is beautiful and productive
-In situations, in actions, and in goods.

Adapt readily to the changing flux of Time
Like a tree swaying in the stormy gales.
Fear neither adversity,
Nor sickness, nor death
Challenge them as far as possible.
Determine your goals
And set your face against the wind.
Overcome!

continued . . .

Give away of your self
And of material goods to others
In particular, to those younger-
But use discretion in this

Think many times
Before you speak
Speak sparingly

Delve deep into the works
Of thinkers around the world
Their collective wisdom
Will nurture your spirit
And enrich your mind.

Be cheerful. Smile a lot
Encourage and appreciate
Those around you
There are certain poisons
Embedded deep
Within a human being
These you eliminate
By dint of constant effort
Win over your self
Master the thing called Mind
Master the thing called Mind!

Sixteen

I have ceased
To be an actor
Waiting for applause
Performing roles for audiences
Uninterested in my portrayals

Now I live only to please my true self
No pretensions, no preening,
No need for praise
From reluctant lips
I wish merely
To prove myself to my self!

I am respectful to another
Because I wish to be
I care for another
Because that is what I like to do
I am kind
Because it makes me
Believe in my humanity
I am considerate
Because that's what pleases me
I am honest
Because falsehood makes me uncomfortable

Seventeen

Time heals, time heals
You flow upon it, you grow
And become a surging wave
That sweeps up to the shore.

How could you break free
Unless you hasten
To torch out the arrogance
Of a self that thrives upon the ego?

Eighteen

Here comes soaring in flight
A flock of black birds,
As I stand upon the roof
And take note.

That dust cloud in the distant woods
Trailing behind the herd of deer
Through which is visible
The flash of silvered-hoof,
And golden coat

These are part of this moment's history
In which the birds, the deer, the cloud
And I, are framed forever.
This moment, that will have
Its impact upon the future
Of everything
Without a doubt remote

Nineteen

I am a dew speck
Clinging to the hyacinth-cup
That blooms in the backyard
Of the house,
That's old, moss grown
And crumbling

The piano whisper of the
Breeze, stirred by the
Blaze in the east
Has woken the weeds
Sprightly, tumbling

I sparkle back at the day
All revelry and solemn notes
All reverberations of the dance
That creation generates
Pass through me
So grand, and so humbling!

Twenty

Every dawn a warbler comes
To warble god knows what
And joy flies in, and pain flies out
In wonder I am caught!

His chirpy flits upon the wall
Are signals sent abroad
That all is well with him and his
That we may rest assured

His monody has signal worth
Far greater than a Man's
Whose monstrous greed
Outstrips his need
Who little understands!

I've known of people troubled by
The give-me-more disease
The more Man gets,
The more he wants
And never seems at ease

continued . . .

The bird fulfills his destiny
By singing to the morn
But Man creates his destiny
By either praise or scorn
Of Life, Creation, and the Power
That manifests the Whole.

This truth, if grasped by humankind
Would halt our frenzied world
From building Babel's tower
And spinning out of control !

Twenty One

No matter how much courage I engender
How many longings I quaff
As with pleasurable taste of wine
How many acts of service I render
For all my flaws sincerely repine
How much endure acts of injustice.
With patience forbear,
With no complaint or whine
Yet, if I am treading a path
Leading merely towards my gloom
My existence would be nothing but vanity

Twenty two

At times I hold my thoughts, arrest them
And listen to the silence speak to me
The voices of my human world
Have ceased their chatter,

While the wind that weaves
Through the trees and the leaves
Begins to speak to me

Each blade of grass,
Each grain of the soil,
All of matter
Is telling me a story
They speak of a glory
Reaching the galaxies
Vanishing
Out and beyond
Imaginable distances
They tell me who I am, and why!
A conscious intelligent speck
Moving from aeon to aeon,
The only one empowered
To consciously create new Universii

Twenty three

For an age I have wandered
Near and far
In search of a Truth
That could stand scrutiny

Perfect, complete, explanatory!!

A voice called out to me
Like Some Philomel's
As I tramped wearily upon
Uninhabited regions wild

Still looking, still seeking
With a mind ill equipped to grasp
The hidden reasons why
I suffered deep sorrow
As though the very earth
Had turned into
A saber toothed pard,
In order to savage me
And I was about to be devoured.

continued . . .

This caller persisted
She sang. Almost whispered
A ditty pulsant, compelling
That swelled in my ear
Until shamed
I bowed before her
And admitted:

The truth is everywhere
Only my eyes were glazed
Only my senses dazed
Darkened by cerebral
Notions of who I am
And wherefore am I

O my deafened ears
O this vision distorted
O the blockage in the
Flow . . . . I had cast away
With both hands,
My own destiny, it appears

Twenty Four

This life that seems eternal to you and me
Is not half a blink in terms of Eternity

Though I wake and sleep
As if I'll live on for ever

I know, I know my days as man
Are few, and utterly fixed my span

True as well, that my essence
Has been around, since Time began

True also that life will follow death
As day follows night

Eternity is strung in pearly moments
Alternately, dark or light

Twenty five

The eye has drowned in longing
To understand True Reality
The gulf between self and the Eternal
Yawns at me

Yet I AM.. and that is the Truth as well
However inadequate the tools
Of word, of thought, of consciousness
With these and my own self
I must vault across

Who else but me,
A human could ever hope
For free access
To the unknown,
The supposedly
Unknowable

Twenty six

I will cry out to every moment of creation
To ignite in you the spark of divinity
Child of my dreams!

When music blends with sight and touch
And cantos flow from voice to air
And the heart of man beats in synch
With Beings of every sort, that share
Their lively ballads, earthly tales
Of joys and woes, dark or fair
Of rainbow-ed skies and misty lands
Textured on the drapes of Time,
With endless skeins of silken strands

My powerful wish must manifest
That you would learn to view with trust
Not put the Truth sublime to test . . .
That the bloom of Life is amaranthine
Now in shadow, now sunshine

Twenty seven

How many thoughts flow
Through my mind,
Like an endless fount?
I could not count

Why did someone appear to be
Attractive and wonderful yesterday
But now seems ordinary, grey?
I could not say

Why do I tread in heaven now?
While last night I lay in hell?
I cannot tell

Twenty eight

The Morning Star has dimmed
Into the silvering blue
A row of hillocks now stands limned
Like a caravan of camels
Arrested in their travel
A sparrow-flock
Springs up from the grass
Resembles a spray of dark gravel

Somewhere among the acacia trees
In the distance
Beyond the emerald wheat fields
A peacock dances
In glorious effulgence

And I look . . . and I listen . . .
To the traveling sounds,
At the traveling star,
At the rising sun,
And this twirling earth
Upon which I stand
Wondering, is this Chance?
I plunge into the silent embrace
Of my solitude in order to find
My true sustenance

Twenty Nine

I stretched out my hand
To grasp the cosmos wholly
It leapt down and swept me upward

I bent an eye of scrutiny

I was the Cosmos entire.
It was and IS me!

Thirty

The tasks are many
And workers few
To right the wrongs
Of our saddened world

I could not leave
My work undone
The flag I bear
Must boldly flutter
Not limply hang on the pole
Crimped and furled

Thirty one

Some sorrow, some pain
There must be
To lend substance
To sunlit spots

But what despair
Is this?
What a destiny
To live in a vault
For a quarter century
With a beast
Who had fathered one?

Some facts are too
Horrendous to be
Dealt with in silence
Or in quiet aversion

What retribution awaits
Our callous race
For letting this pass

Thirty two

With carefree gait
I'd bend my feet
To greet the day!
I'd satiate
Upon its splendid lay

I'd spread my arms
The earth embrace
In an expansive
Ecstatic blaze

I'd swing the
Pendulum of Time
As it were, a mighty bell

I'd kiss an atom
Wink at a quark
In the brevity
Of its weeny spell

continued . . .

I'd freely lark
With scruffy crows,
Carefree as a fainéant

Make grand
Outlandish plans,
Then doze
Beside an ancient
Monument

I'd gladly be a mendicant
And sing and dance
To celebrate
Life's exotic minutiae
As well as its enormity

Thirty three

In the mornings at six o clock
The world invades my sanctuary
A daily lacerating japer
In the rolled up plop
Of the newspaper
Which I unroll hungrily

The fare is spread before me
Like a meal for a beast:
Murder, rape, disaster
And politicians with their
Meretricious caper!

Thirty four

In 50 years
What was aglitter
To begin with,
Has lost its sheen

What was ugly
Is comfortably acceptable

Those who were in servitude
Are lords of manors

Those who were eminent
Have lived their lives
Climbed the heights
And have now descended
Into ordinariness

Foreign shores are no longer enticing.

The moon is merely
A few days' rocket journey away

The white, black, yellow faces
Have become easily distinguishable

The humble have turned
Into movie stars
The Moguls of yesteryears are forgotten

continued . . .

He who seemed so handsome
Appears to be frumpy and queerly outdated

The nimble footed have slowed
The songs and melodies have jazzed up
Empires have vanished
Nations fragmented
New ones created too

The rainbow, when it appears
Is a quiet spectacle
Its romance has been wiped out

Countless gusts of wind
Have ruffled the surfaces
Of rivers and seas
That continue changing
But seem unchanged

Kings and queens are no more awesome
Parents are just beautiful memories

However, I am here grown aware,
That my life is a mystic marvel
That re-invents its self in accord
With my whims,
In tireless pursuit of perfecting me

Thirty five

It has been a long vigil
The cranes have flown
Back to Siberia
And winter with its chill
Long nights is gustily
In retreat

The planets whirl
Unceasingly
But I am stationary, still.
Possessed by a thought-

That I am centric
To creation
That all knowledge
Indeed, the Cosmos itself
Radiates from my will

If "I" were not sentient
All this empyrean grandeur
Could not be present

Thirty six

I am neither an atom nor a galaxy
Just an ordinary human being
I understand there's power
Unimaginable in any star
And that the atomic world
Of mysterious particles
When it is by scientists tweaked
And at a target hurled
To smithereens a city, can blow
All this I know.

I am a conscious event
And carry the inexplicable
Burden of awareness!

Foolish notion, I agree
But difficult to rid
That everything is there
And I am here
All alone—
In Matter's Middle Zone

Thirty seven

When the summer-fall
Began to gild the side walk
With amber leaves
Pithering from above

The trees stood bare
Their boughs like
Scimitars guarding
A secret trove

It was then my heart
Refreshed, I waited
For the emerald buds
To re-adorn the grove

New leaves were soon aflutter
And robin, crow and sparrow
For supremacy
Upon the branches strove

Oh Life inexhaustible
You are a mystery!
Yet visible and worthy
Of my adoration and my love

Thirty eight

I desire-

Not to lose myself, loving another.
Yet, to love with such depth that
The one upon whom I gaze
Begins to glow with my loving
And retains it forever
While my own heart's
Satiated with this giving

Thirty nine

Let me hold each moment
Like an infant newly born
With all its promises intact

A speck of Time holding
Within it the magnitude
Of eternity

I am not here
Merely to exist . . . then vanish
Like a flicker
On a TV screen

I am the creator of the whole
One who has been
Always a seeker of the Truth

Words fail to express
My quintessential worth
Portentous as a monarch
Who proclaims as his own
The entire earth

Forty

Like butterflies, my desires!
Like passing clouds
Like heaving seas
Like shimmering trees
In summer storms

The promises to self
I thought I'd carry through
The teeming youthful fantasies
That seemed so achievable and true
Today stand embarrassingly stark
Like harvested peanut haulms!

Forty one

My wandering feet
Took me to a bamboo grotto
Drawn I was within its stockade
Of light green stems
Packed in a perfect circle

I gazed for a while
At its sandy floor
Brown, grey, and brindled
As if a fox had wagged
Its bushy tail across it

Not a bird's twitter,
Nor buzz of fly or honey bee
Were there to greet me

My sense of self slowly
Dwindled
For the grotto was silent and still
Resembling some abandoned
Ancient citadel

continued . . .

Then a single leaf began to quiver
Like a tuning fork.

I readied myself for communion
Spirit to Spirit
A message was conveyed:
"I am one with the life force
O human!
In harmony do I dwell with every thing
Timeless as the earth from which I spring
I am not too easily swayed.

You who wander about like an aimless
Drifting bubble
Your days you spend
Seeking succor, avoiding trouble
What do you do you here?"

I reached up and caressed the
Speaking leaf
I spoke to it of my own belief

continued . . .

That sentience
Has, in a sense
Made me different
That it is my destiny
To be adrift
To endure loss and pain
In order to understand
The Truth of existence

This distance
from the creative source
Is only seeming!
That I am taking care
To bridge the gap
And in this striving
Is the fulfillment
Of which perhaps
You leaf, are merely dreaming

Forty two

You'd be amazed to learn, my child
That you mean poetry and song to me!

A mysterious process prompted
By the self
Meandering through
Uncharted alleyways of worlds
Imaginary
Then encountering
Some sharp anguish or another
I am propelled towards
My own spirit

Then and then alone
The strains I hear
Of a celestial sound
A musical balm,
Soothing and calm
It is then that words flutter
Like dozing doves,
Startled by a shot!
Resettle in harmony
Upon the page
And a song is born

Forty three

A poly-bag
Along the railway track
Hops in the winds
Resembling a crow
With broken wings

A geriatric
Like a half filled sack
Desperately clings
To the train bar
Wonders where'd his
Youthful vigor go?

Browned poly-bag no one owns

Fribble of an old baggabones

Forty four

Have you sister, taken a ceremonial bath
In the pellucid pond (where the willows weep),
That lies, shivering in ecstasy
Beneath the drizzle of rain
Its liquid heart exposed, wide and deep?

And have you now broken
Your woman's bonds
By opening up your inner self
To the spirit of all things visible
And so shattered the myth risible
That you are but a dumb
Portrait on the shelf?

You are in fact strong and free
You've gazed at your reflection
And seen with clarity
Your own potency!

Forty five

I will not be cowed down
By the whim-whams of life
Like a lion I'll roar

A Problem? I will nail it
A Mountain? I will scale it
An Ocean? I will sail it
What are ships for?

Trouble – I'd embrace you
For the friend that your are
You bring out the steel in me
Potent and vigorous
Is the zeal in me
No trouble could mar
The joy I feel in me

Forty six

This is not a simple missive,
Not merely words on paper
It is the heart felt benediction,
Of my spiritual father!
How deeply penetrative of my spirit
How thunderously reverberate!
The prayer of a man for his paining daughter
From the Mentor for a disciple losing her grip

When the winds blow sharp and threatening
I hold this piece of paper close
And gaze at it to comfort myself

When I falter in my strides
Towards the goal
I cling to this message
And somehow my heart ceases its
Dirge and beats with a new rhythm
Composed, steady, firm, resolved

Forty seven

The Peace, that leaders talk of
With such intensity
Words of hope!
Ah!! hope undefined

The frolicsome wind
Will carry the sound
Of their voices
Towards the next clump
Of palm trees
Convert it into a whisper
And move on

Time will flow, as will
The rivers and the tides
The seagulls will wheel
And alight, and fly off again

And the solitary scop
Will gaze into the distance
And will miss by a whisker
The call of peace
And he will wonder and frown
In perplexity, why hope
Had stirred in his heart
And why it had vanished

Forty eight

The lime plastered walls
Of the backyard seem to be
Melting in the sun's light
Like blocks of ice, milky white

I touch the walls
And through them
The sun's beneath my hand
Surprisingly chill at first,
Then warming up, enfolding me

My mind's in suspension
A certainty overtakes me
That everything around
Is holding me
Firm in its attention
Urging me to lift myself up
To lift myself up and soar away

Forty nine

We have moved ahead of Lawrence
Everyone who reads has read
The sagacious outpourings
Of the last two hundred years
All philosophical treatises
And even Summum Bonum

Though the idea has
Percolated our consciousness
That Life Force exists
It has lost its novelty
It has been tossed aside
As another mystic hokum

Yet I am prompted
To uncover layer by layer
Life's marvelous breadth
Its yang and yin
The power of death
The entire existential sum

continued . . .

I must keep returning to it
Be moved, be thrilled
Exalted . . . and soberly
Its abundance plumb
For it satisfies that part
Of me which I often neglect
To nurture . . . . in myself
In the daily hum and drum.

Fifty

To My Human Other
Despite the rocky arete
That at places comes between,
You and I are not disparate
Across barriers, thoughts have flown

Your sadness and your despair
Find a gauzy home within me
Where they lodge like fledglings bare
Afraid, atremble, alone

But then your laughter rumbles
Too, come rolling in to me
And for reasons unknown,
A joy tickles and tumbles
Until I feel the vibrations
In the marrow of every bone

Fifty one

Oftentimes I look up
And draw you
Upon myself
Like a sequined veil
There seems to be
An indefinable
Pull between us

You never fail
To rivet me

Bent upon arriving
At their nameless
Destinations,
Motor drivers on the streets
Insulated within small
Bubble worlds,
Intently train their
Eyes upon the macadam
Which like a livid serpent
Slithers unendingly underneath

continued . . .

Your brilliantine weave
Merits but a passing thought
A careless glance
The bridal finery
With which you pulsate
Fiery as a sun spot
To them is a barely visible dance

I imagine you have forever pined
For the attentions of Mankind
Like an elderly mom
Waiting for a smile
From her busy-bee son

I am all yours though
Am I consolation enough?

Fifty two

My physical self is all alone
Except you, in your darkness
Blazing with uncountable eyes
Gazing at me!

So, there is acceptance
So, the silence that steals
Upon the rows of colonies
Binds me more securely
To your vastness

Did I say 'alone'?
But far from a desolate wail
There springs a buoyant
Certainty of immanence
It strikes up the chords
Of a quiet barcarole

I see the entire
World absorbing me
Even as I pervade the whole

Fifty three

Mountains of verbiage
A cacophonous eruption

Man's amazing power
Of language!!
Truly a blueprint
For the ways of Creation
Unceasing, unstoppable
Evolving fluxion

What caprice then
Makes me yearn
For a silent veldt
Devoid of sound
Except the sough
of wind, Hushed
and quiescent
Where the silence
Will not be shattered
By any enunciation

Fifty four

A god is hidden within your glance
In your steady gaze dwells eternity
Although your ears
Are harmlessly settled
Upon your crown
Like two concaved cactus leaves
The slight twitch hurls me a warning
That you are alert

The ferocious whiskers
Seem subdued by your subtle smile

This quiet subordination
At variance with your
Sejant pose mocks the
Hunter in Man

Who 'shoots' you anyway
This time
With his video cam

Fifty five

Mynahs, a couple of them
With their squawks and blatter
Fluttering leaves of the laburnum
Dotted with its buds of chrome

Around the M.C's fountain
Kids splurge and splatter
I crane my neck to watch them
Through the darkening gloam

Within me begins to stream
A happy sense of freedom
That expands and spreads
Like a flock of starlings
Hurrying towards their home

Fifty six

What magnetic field in me
Draws you close
You truly are everywhere
busily doing what needs be done

A kite is screeching
In piteous hunger
Perched upon a leafless
Silk cotton tree
Though it's invisible to me

I marvel at your ability
To fit a dying star
Into a black hole
Be at once of cosmic size
Be just as comfortable
Confined in a nucleus !

continued . . .

I can imagine it, the kite
Breathtakingly beautiful
In its need for aliment
It waits, as I too do
For some response
To its cry, then it screams anew

I add my petition to hers
And am startled
By the swoop of feathers
My half eaten pie flies
Under her claws!

Fifty seven

Neither my awareness of me
Nor my presence in this world
Is Reality. Some say it is incidental

Though at times
I stand with puzzled brow
Untangling the weft and woof

In order to drive away the chaos
To discover grace and my place
In the scheme of things

I am the power that permeates
Time and Space
I am death and I am breath
No 'being' I know of, is
Better equipped to
Understand the Truths

continued . . .

For the truths are many
Not necessarily a single one
And even as I strive to learn
The essence of something
It promptly changes
Its self, transforms
So that I no longer
Know it
I am like a child
Grasping at soap bubbles

Fifty eight

The eternal Spirit
Calls us to love !!
I can love the very germs
The slithering worms
The slimy slugs
And stinging bugs

I am connected with every thing
Dependent on everything
And on every one
From a single source
We spring
Like rays from the sun

Yet I am broken
Each day, fragmented
By a hideous
Sense of isolation

continued . . .

Shrouded by a
Darkness that inhabits
The world

A mad scramble
For mirages of gold
A Faustian urge in
All of us to gain
The glitter
And in the process
Our eternal
Serenity we have sold

Fifty nine

This boulder overlooks
The valley of Doon
A sumo wrestling with the wind!
A young female stands upon it
Lifts up her face to the heavens
And stabs the sky
With her finger
Then she leaps,
Plummets to the valley floor

And is lost to my view
The shock is
Like a snake bite
That darkens my vision
For a long while

But the boulder
Stands stolidly, unperturbed
By the foolishness of love

Sixty

We are scattered
Like droplets
Falling upon hard surfaces

Not even the solid cadences
Of a symphony
Could have gathered together
The man who has plugged
His ears, and now sits
Enclosed in a room

He could go out and
Walk among the
Crowds, or join the drummers;
He sends out his ghost instead

This fractioning of self
Further withholds the unity
He dreams of attaining

continued . . .

No, he must leap across
Travel beyond the tunnels of
Ignorance,
Across the dark landscape,
Then may be
The sky would yield its secret
And tease away the synapses
Built through foolish yearnings
A human's essence is all light
He must acknowledge it
And reconnect with the Power
From whence he has sprung

Sixty one

Where does one truly live?
In words and ideas
Our own or those of men,
Dead a long time ago?

Or is living like
A charade I watch
Through a glassy wall,
Cold and clear as a crystal ball?
I happen to love
That part of life
More intensely
When I connect
With everything

Yet often I am
Separated, and isolated
From it all

Sixty two

I AM whatever I make of self at any given time
Strange, I am so many things, so many shades
So many personalities—I am peopled by a world.

Are they the yet-to-be-born beings?
Or are they phantoms from my past.?
The infinite number of persons I have been or will be,
All living together, neatly fitted in me, in this moment?
The slow as a sloth is the one dominating others now, but
I wait for the silver fish, the koel-smart one to overtake soon.
It is entirely possible, and why not?
I did not invite Ms sloth-bear
To come reside as the VIP in hotel ME.

Sixty three

I, me, human, nameless
You, Creation, universe, endless
I and you, do we have a history?
A once upon a time . . . . in Time?
Are we two antipodal entities
Pitted against each other?
Or are we interchangeable
Like the earth's magnetic poles?
Both existing IN each other
Never wholly apart
Yet distinct

Sixty four

The radiant vigor of life
Yes, of LIFE!!
Press it upon the
Hope-dead , the blind-sophists
The spirit emptied ones

Those who in the midst
of their frantic activity
Are merely waiting to merge
Into the gentler vibrations of death
A tear for their emptiness
One pained sigh for
Hearts heavy with folly

Sixty five

We exist like fish in a dark, dark ocean
Where every encounter spells danger
Where selfishness, is ready to devour us
We live in a world sliding into bestiality.

Day by day the news gets murkier
We each of us struggle to live with dignity
Beneath the crushing weight
Amidst the stench of greed, arrogance, egoism
Hoping all would go well with us and ours.

That is a chimera, being shattered daily
In millions of lives across the globe

continued . . .

This our beautiful blue planet
Is like a penitentiary for souls
Who are lost to the correct way of life
What can sustain us then?
I believe it is only the circle
Of people who cherish us
Who care for our well being with sincerity
Who would suffer with us and share our
Pain and sorrow as if it is their own
Who would stand by us, not counting the cost
Who would lay down their life for our sake
Who would not complain when we fall short
Those who wish to bring only joy into our lives

No matter how inadequate they seem
Or how troublesome they may be at times
I would go down on my knees
With gratitude for having
Such friends in my life

Sixty six

We cannot leave you
For you are pervasive
We try to grasp you
As if you were solid
Oh this ceaseless grasping!

Cocooned in my
Infantile understanding
I wait for fusion more
Complete than can
Be expressible

This so far is our story
This un-assuaged thirst
This living on the edge
Of the now and the never

No ethereal beings
Could replace
My image in the mirror
The one I've come to love,
I wholly belong to her
Created by her
From moment to moment
For ever

Sixty seven

On Peace

Peace comes to me with your smiles
Like the sun shining across the miles

It is in your warmth as my brother
It is in your caring acts
In the tear you swallow
When my grief you embrace
In the joy on your face
When I am winning my race

It is simply your human response
To me and to every Other
I speak not for my lone self
Nor of you as a single person
For you and I and every one
Are we all, not seeking bliss?

Not a complex process, this
It requires no cogitations
No pompous committees
Treaties or negotiations

continued . . .

We just need to break thru
A shell in which we each are trapped
The shell of selfishness we nurture
The untrammeled cravings
For power and for pelf
The insularity and unconcern
For anyone except our own self
Or even for our own future
This bestiality will devour us all
Including the empowered ones
Together we will fall!

The trivialities to which we apportion
Our days need to be examined
This living for the moment
As if death is a mythical notion
Disbelief in the Eternity of life
I am certain, is at the root
Of our distorted ways

We are hurtling
We are hurtling
Along a glitzy maze
Down towards a horrible place

continued . . .

Lest this tends to intimidate
Take a look at the headlines
And ponder how the ugly exposure
Has turned you insensate

We can heal the world of misery
The sages have shown us the way
Let's get strong in ourselves
First cleanse out our minds
Of all traces of ego and greed
Be at peace within
Next tackle the sickness prevailing
With gentle persuasion
With genuine concern
Treating each man as an equal
Listening to each one's story
Laying the foundations of trust
For the sake of our children
Say 'Yes' to peace we must.

Sixty eight

They've sung their songs
Some of love, or pain
Or of wishful dreams

Their songs have laughed or grieved
For friend, or for a lover dead
And spoken with longing
Of some god and of a heaven

Delighted in moonlit mists
And languid streams
They have gazed with
Grave intensity
At the vastness of the azure seas and sky
Sought to learn its how and why.

continued . . .

Heralded an age that limned
The forest edge with hope,
Then resorted to mocking
The folly of Man
At times they've come close
To proclaiming that
The answers are losing
Their way amidst the dust and noise

The poets have left my big question
Looming like a pendulum
About to strike:
If men are ignorant of the value
Of their life,
What would transform the world?

Sixty nine

Some bard claims he is trespassing
Upon the earth!
Like an alien

He stops to listen to the sharp
Crackle of dry leaves
That flutter bravely in the winter gusts.

Like Kirkegaard he believes
And whispers to himself that
There is None; No one at all
With whom he could establish kinship
Yet Dryad like he walks
Through the silent, chilly street
His very pores alert to change

Seventy

There is nothing noteworthy
Within the pages of many a book
Except old recycled dribble
Penned by those with time on hands
Who like me—scribble

Seventy one

I could plunge myself deep
Deeper still as if beneath
The rolling billows,
I am in search of a lost city

Or hack my way
To the heart of the forest
Where perhaps the solitude of
Self, glorying in its consciousness
Enunciates the healing
Of my maladies
Where I would like to dwell
And let my poesy bloom

Seventy two

In the lightening gloom
When bulbuls and thrushes
Trilling rejoice, safely hidden
In dark dense bushes,
Not exposed on electric poles
And the dove and koel
Somewhere far off
Do not hesitate
To make their call
A gecko waddles up
Looks around and stares

I miss the lizard on the wall
That is at home behind
The tube light, where it flicks
At the fly or crawls and
Makes its love call
As if a strip of paper tears

Stilled by their quiet wisdom
I pause to reflect that the
Everlasting cycle is reassuring.
Firmly on life, Nature has its grip
Have I cast aside the very things that
Caused me deep joy
Connecting me with the spirit
Pulsing in creation and lost myself
In foolish Mammon worship?

Seventy three

Everywhere I go I hear it whispered
Breathed so softly, that the words
Slip into my ears like moles
I thought it happens in my land alone
But amazingly it is thriving
Elsewhere as well

People are busy, they work
To strive seems to be
Written in our genes
At the end of it all
Stand in a belligerent row
Bills, rentals, mortgaged homes

Bound, enslaved, disempowered
We have no money, we are tight
Where is freedom?
The only ones who seem comfortable
And well off are government employees
The world over

Seventy four

It walks with me wherever I go,
Neither a shadow
Nor a graspable presence
It sits in silence by my elbow
Waiting for me to turn my head
I close my twin eyes
And try to see this
One, who is inseparable from my self
Without whom I am hollow
As a drum
As repetitively pointless
As the ball being dribbled
By the child on the floor below

Somehow I have lost contact
With my essence
Somehow I have had the notion
That I've been moving to and fro
Like a pendulum marking time
Between my first breath, and death
Assuring my self: this is life
This ability to navigate
With my physical senses
Through time and space
Meanwhile the invisible One
My True self innate
Waits with infinite
Patience, for my awakening

Seventy five

A summer leaf makes a landing
In my courtyard
Its deltoid amber blade
Seared by the sun
Drifts and bobs awhile
Indecisive
Then it seems to have found
The most appropriate spot
Settles upon it
And begins to swing
With the breeze

My chest swells up!
With a surge of empathy
I welcome her into my self

Seventy six

A song

The words . . . of the Mentor are pearls—are pearls
Open your heart . . . hold them there, seal them
Trust that the truth
Grand visions unfurls
Its mysteries are deeper than you feel them
Open your heart . . . hold them there, seal them

When karma unfolds in sickness and pain
Strengthen your faith
The power of Daimoku will heal them

The words of the Mentor are pearls . . . are pearls
Open your heart . . . hold them there, seal them
Trust that the truth
Grand visions unfurls
Its mysteries are deeper than you feel them
Open your heart . . . hold them there, seal them

continued . . .

As the joy of the Law
Wells up within
Every moment you'll treasure
Each Day it's a pleasure
Just to be live

You will win . . . you will win

The words of the Mentor are pearls . . . are pearls
Open your heart . . . hold them there, seal them

Trust that the truth . . . .

Seventy seven

A song

The Universe is listening with tender care
It's paying heed . . . . to every need . . . that I declare
The Universe is listening with care.

The sum total of me . . . is . . . . .like an instant message sent
To every atom everywhere

The Universe . . . . .

I am the Hero, . . . of the play I penned
I will enact, the script I wrote
That no one else can share

Performance is mine alone . . . . endurance is mine alone

The Universe . . . . .is listening with care
The Universe . . . .

How things work out, which ever way they go
I must believe, the power lies . . . . within me
. . . . To chart out my course

continued . . .

The driver's seat, is mine indeed
The Master-Mind, innate in all

Is Time, is Space, is Life's very force

It is the ocean wide . . . .
My role is just to sail along
Its mighty, powerful tide.

Compliance is mine alone . . . . .accordance is mine alone

The Universe . . . .

Seventy eight

A song
I am no longer buffeted
By the storms on
Mighty oceans
Or on the land

I have stepped on the road
Towards building a new dawn

My life moves like a swan
On a tranquil summer morn

I am a pacifist . . . I have a dream

There will rise, there will grow

A force to free the world
Of the misery of war

The sentinels of peace
Will multifold increase

continued . . .

The sentinels of peace
Will multifold increase

Dance with Joy . . . . .
Dance with joy

They'll turn the saha world
Into a land of bliss

They'll break the bondages
To bring about release
Now is the time . . . . this is the day

Of a total Vic..To..Ry!!

Seventy nine

Be the king . . . of your l..ife
Touch that star, in the dawning hour
Holding the reins of your morrows
Speeding with power you are

When you strive
Ever more
Following the way of the Mentor
Based on the Truth of the Law

No regrets . . . . no sorrows
Will you carry to the other shore

Be the king of your life
You've got a destiny in store
Touch that star in the dawning hour
Holding the reins of your morrows
Speeding with power you are

As you toil every day
Awakening to your true calling
Sweeping your troubles aside

The bird within the cage and birds without
Will to one another find their way
Be the king of you life
Touch that star . . . .

About the Poet

Ms Sushma Sagar has been penning poems since childhood. This is her second collection of poems. The first collection, "The Beggar woman and Other Poems" was published in 2002.

Sushma has been in turn an educator, a copywriter, and a journalist. She worked for The National Herald as a correspondent in Mumbai. She gravitated towards activism during her association with the YWCA in the eighties and nineties, during which time she actively fought for the cause of justice in society alongside such well known crusaders like Medha Patkar

For the past decade she has been mainly occupied in writing and learning about Buddhism.

She lives in Chandigarh, India.